Test Bank

for

Johnson and Johnson

Joining Together
Group Theory and Group Skills

Sixth Edition

prepared by

James M. Mitchell
University of Minnesota

David W. Johnson
University of Minnesota

Allyn and Bacon
Boston · London · Toronto · Sydney · Tokyo · Singapore

Chapter 1

Objectives:

After finishing this chapter students should be able to:

1) Define and explain exactly what a group is.

2) Understand the role of groups in human history.

3) Explain all the components of group dynamics and how in-group interactions can impact group effectiveness.

4) Understand how each group member is individually accountable to the other group members if the group is to be truly effective.

5) Understand and explain how social norms can impact group functioning.

6) Explain the difference in achieved outcomes between a group with high interpersonal interdependence and low interpersonal interdependence.

Summary:

From the beginnings of history, humans have functioned better when they live and work in small groups. History has shown that the Cro-Magnons (from whom we humans have evolved) survived the ice age because they lived and traveled in groups. Groups have impacted human history ever since, and for anyone to be truly successful, in life or just in business, a knowledge of group dynamics is essential.

A group is a number of individuals who join together in order to achieve a common goal. Usually, a group consists of a number of individuals who are <u>interdependent</u>, that is they rely upon each other in some way. Most often, group members interact with each other on a regular basis. Members often perceive themselves as members of the group and their interactions are usually structured by a set of **roles** and **norms**. Each individual in the group may influence the other group members, and the joint association may exist in order to satisfy a mutual need.

Some groups function more effectively than others. A **pseudogroup** is a group whose members have been assigned to work together, but who have no interest in doing so. These groups usually function at a very low level of effectiveness. A **traditional work group** is a group whose members agree to work together, but see little benefit in doing so. These groups function at a somewhat higher, but still moderate, level of effectiveness. Rather, an **effective group** is a group whose members commit themselves to the common purpose of maximizing their own and each other's success. These groups often function at a very high level of effectiveness.

Usually, members of an effective group have specific roles. The group's common beliefs, norms, dictate member behavior. Norms are often developed out of interactions among members of the group. **Positive interdependence** focuses on the "We are all in this together" concept. Individuals in the group succeed only if the group as a whole succeeds. Each member of an effective group is **individually accountable** to the other group members. An effective group allows for **social skill** development, so that members may communicate with each other in a **face-to-face** format. Effective groups also allow for **group processing**, in order for group members to reflect on and evaluate both individual and group performance. Hence, there is a discipline for creating group productivity.

Kurt Lewin was one of the pioneers in the development of **group dynamics** theory. He sought to develop theories which could be applied to real world social problems. He coined the term action research, research which could lead to practical solutions. Much of Lewin's research highlighted the importance of active participation in groups in order to learn new skills, develop new attitudes, and obtain new knowledge about groups. His work, more than anyone else's, shows the interrelationships between knowledge about group dynamics and actual small group skills.

Activities:

1.1 Your Solitary Activities p. 7
1.2 Who am I ? p. 8
1.3 What Is A Group? p. 8
1.4 Are Groups Beneficial Or Harmful?
1.5 Developing an Effective Group p. 34

Short-Answer Essay Questions:

1) What is a group?

2) How have small groups influenced human history?

3) What are the components of a high-level functioning group?

4) What is a reference group?

5) Why is interdependence important for small group effectiveness?

6) Describe the work of Kurt Lewin and its importance on the field of group dynamics.

7) How does small group involvement impact psychological health?

8) How can group members assess overall group functioning?

9) What is experiential learning?

10) What is a role conflict?

Multiple Choice:

1) A role is
a)   assignment to a position within a larger group.
b)   a behavior defining one occupant's position to another.*
c)   portraying one character within a small group.
d)   one person in the group speaking while the others listen.

2) Status refers to
a)   popularity within the group.
b)   group achievement.
c)   one group member's power within the group.*
d)   a social norm.

3) A role conflict is
a) deciding who has priority in each small group.
b) differing expectations or obligations for specific group members.*
c) two group members agreeing to disagree.
d) two group members quarreling over achieved outcomes.

4) A norm is
a) a group-established rule to regulate membership behavior.*
b) a rule applying to all groups in an activity.
c) a tool for measuring group success.
d) not a necessary component of an effective group.

5) Group dynamics is
a) an idea of how people interact with one another.
b) the scientific study of behavior in groups.*
c) important to the study of individual activity.
d) solely related to competition and achievement.

6) In effective groups
a) members influence each other on the basis of expertise.
b) members flexibly match decision-making procedures with situation needs.
c) members engage in creative controversy.
d) all of the above.*

7) Self-efficacy is
a) the expectation that success will be achieved through personal effort.*
b) individual group members handling put-downs.
c) a group member's desire to lead the group.
d) one group member giving in to the opinions of the other group member.

8) Effective groups exhibit
a) periodic interdependence.
b) individual accountability.*
c) group selection.
d) all of the above.

9) Group processing may be defined as
a) reflecting on a group session in order to improve both individual and overall group performance.*
b) group members offering constructive criticisms of each other.
c) everybody receiving a "high-five".
d) thanking the other group members for their contributions.

10) Creating group productivity requires
a) one member taking charge.
b) discipline.*
c) group members coming to a quick agreement.
d) competition among group members.

Terms:

aggregate
conflict of interests
effective group
Goals
Group
group dynamics
group processing
group structure
high-performance group
individual accountability
Interdependence
Interpersonal Interaction
learning contract
Lewin
means interdependence
norm
outcome interdependence
positive interdependence
primary group
process goals
promotive interaction
pseudogroup
recurring-phase theories
role
role conflict
sequential-stage theories
small group
social skill development
status
traditional work group

Chapter 2

Objectives:

After reading this chapter students should be able to:

1) Understand the concept of experiential learning and begin to develop quality-centered small group skills.

2) Understand how the eight steps of learning group skills can impact a small group's achievement of a desired outcome.

3) Understand how action theory affects small group dynamics.

4) Develop a relationship between the concept of encouraging small groups to succeed and achieving such success.

5) Understand how role playing in a small group can help achieve a higher-quality group decision.

Summary:

Procedural learning involves a progressive refinement of knowledge and skill as the procedures are practiced, practiced, and practiced. In other words, this book focuses on both "head" and "hand" learning. Experiential learning begins with the formulation of an action theory. Action theories specify what actions are needed in order to achieve a desired sequence in a given situation. The next step is to take action and engage in the relevant group skills. The success or failure of the action is assessed. Upon reflection, the action theory is refined and re-formulated. Group skills are then used again in a modified and improved manner. This cycle is repeated continually as skills are refined and improved. Such continuous improvement eventually results in expertise in the use of group skills as changes in cognitive understanding, attitudes, and behavioral patterns result. Psychological success results from such experiential learning. Participant observation also enables one to know when to use various group skills and how to help others to do so in order to improve overall group functioning.

Short-Answer Essay Questions:

1) What is a good way to design a good skill-training session?

2) What is meant by the term participant-observer?

3) Why is role-playing important to good small group development?

4) What are the twelve principles to gaining expertise through experiential learning?

5) What is meant by action theory?

6) What is meant by procedural learning?

7) What is meant by the term evaluation?

8) What impacts how a group coordinator conducts a session?

9) Why is experiential learning important in achieving psychological success?

Multiple Choice:

1) procedural learning involves
a)   feedback about performance.*
b)   one person taking charge in the group.
c)   all group members adopting each perspective.
d)   a strong study of theory before any skill training activity may commence.

2) Action theory determines that groups must possess
a)   no prejudices whatsoever.
b)   a desired outcome or consequence.*
c)   alternative aspirations for success.

d)   a true acceptance for one another.

3) Experiential learning relies heavily on
a)   facilitator/participant interaction.
b)   continuous refinement of the process.*
c)   stimulus/touch learning.
d)   changing attitudes over time.

4) The critical step in learning group skills is to
a)   understand the theoretical concepts thoroughly.
b)   understand how expertise affects guided practice.
c)   understand why the skill is important and its potential personal value.*
d)   know how to scaffold.

5) Motivation is based on learning goal perception and the
a)   need to have goals fit the outcomes.
b)   method use to accomplish such goals.
c)   ability to change group perceptions.
d)   desire to associate such perceptions with skill-building exercises.*

6) Role playing is vital for
a)   action theories.
b)   ethical practice.
c)   experiential learning.*
d)   all of the above.

7) The more effective the role playing
a)   the more learning that can occur.
b)   the better the understanding of perspectives.
c)   the stronger the development of communication skills.
d)   all of the above.*

8) Observation procedures
a)   provide for a good visual demonstration.*
b)   give the facilitator a break.
c)   allow group members to interact with members from another group.
d)   all of the above.

9) One element of a good skill-training session is
a)   repeated use of the exercise.*
b)   participant turn-taking.
c)   a hidden agenda.
d)   all of the above.

10) Which of the following are characteristics of democratic groups?
a)   less repressed hostility.
b)   less scapegoating.
c)   increased member satisfaction.
d)   all of the above.*

Terms:

Action Theory
Ethics
Evaluation
Experiential Learning
Observation Procedures
Process Observation
Role Playing
Skill Training

Chapter 3

Objectives:

Class members should be able to define and discuss in a salient knowledgeable manner the following concepts:

1. Goal
2. Group goal
3. Social interdependence
4. Operational goal
5. Hidden agenda
6. Cooperation
7. Goal structure
8. Competition
9. Individualistic efforts
10. Distributive justice
11. Merit system
12. Equality system
13. Need system
14. Level of aspiration

Summary:

Groups exist for a reason. People join groups to achieve goals they are unable to achieve by themselves. The personal goals of individual group members are linked together by positive interdependence. Group goals result. Group goals direct, channel, motivate, coordinate, energize, and guide the behavior of group members. To be useful, however, group goals have to be clear and operational. The group level of aspiration is continually being revised on the basis of success and failure.

The basis for the group goals is the positive interdependence among group members. Social interdependence theory originated from Kurt Lewin's field theory and was formalized by Morton Deutsch. In the past 90 years over 600 studies have been conducted. The numerous variables that are affected by cooperation may be subsumed within three broad and interrelated outcomes: Effort to achieve, quality of relationships among participants, and psychological health and social competence. Within cooperative groups, as opposed to competitive and individualistic efforts, achievement is higher, committed and caring relationships form, and the self-esteem and social competence required to cope with stress and adversity. Each of these outcomes affect the others. The more group members work together to get the job done, the more members care about each other. The more members care about each other, the harder they work to get the job done. The more group members work together to get the job done, the greater their social competencies and psychological health become. The healthier they are psychologically, the harder they will work to get the job done. The more caring and supportive the relationships, the greater the psychological health and the greater the psychological health the more caring and support individuals can give to each other. When individuals join into a cooperative effort, the whole gestalt results. Finally, while group members will have cooperative, competitive, and individualistic goals, the cooperative goals must dominate. The cooperative effort to achieve group goals requires frequent, clear, and accurate communication. Group members must be able to communicate and listen clearly and effectively.

Activities:

3.1 Orientations Toward social Interdependence
3.2 Are Group Goals Necessary?
3.3 Your Goal-related Behavior
3.4 Clear and Unclear Goals
3.5 Plane Wreck
3.6 Broken Squares
3.7 Cooperative, Competitive, and Individualistic Goal Structures
3.8 Subsistence
3.9 Your Cohesion Behavior
3.10 The Level of Acceptance in your Group
3.11 How Trusting and Trustworthy Am I?
3.12 Practicing Trust Building Skills
3.13 Open Versus Closed Relationships

Short-Answer Essay Questions:

1) What is a goal and how does it pertain to a small group's purpose?

2) What is meant by social interdependence?

3) Cite specific outcomes of social interdependence.

4) Why is social interdependence important to small group functioning?

5) How is cooperative interdependence achieved in a small group?

6) Explain the impact of rewards on small group social interdependence.

7) Explain the relationship between small group social interdependence and the "real world".

8) How are goals related to social interdependence?

9) What is trust and how is it developed in a small group?

10) How is trust related to social interdependence in a small group?

Multiple Choice:

1) Groups form for
a) a purpose.*
b) a cause.
c) a diversion from ordinary activities.
d) financial gain.

2) A goal is
a) an ideal.*
b) not necessary for successful group functioning.
c) sometimes necessary for successful group functioning.
d) often helpful in order to establish group identity.

3) Group goals must be

a) clearly understood.*
b) related to the structured interdependence of the group members.
c) of a passionate nature.
d) all of the above.

4) Group goals
a) require facilitator involvement.
b) direct group behavior.*
c) should be broad and all-encompassing.
d) all of the above.

5) Goals should be
a) clear.*
b) prioritized.
c) helpful for all session participants.
d) often repeated during sessions.

6) Specific steps which are not readily seen in achieving an ideal are referred to as
a) hidden goals.*
b) coercive goals.
c) co-goals.
d) achievement goals.

7) When group members are affected by other group members, the outcome is called
a) experiential learning.
b) social interdependence.*
c) positive influence.
d) co-dependency.

8) Social interdependence originally evolved from
a) Asch's theory of influence.
b) Lewin's field theory.*
c) Deutsch's theory of bargaining.
d) Deutsch's work on conflict.

9) Working together in order to accomplish shared goals is known as
a) cooperation.*
b) unionism.*
c) competition.
d) individualism.

10) Interpersonal trust is established and developed when group members
a) maintain their individual points of view no matter what.
b) take risks and advocate their positions.
c) listen to opposing perspectives and re-state what they hear.
d) b and c.*

Terms:

cathexis
competition
competitive goal structure
cooperation
cooperative goal structure
cooperative intentions
critical path method
distributive justice
equality system
equity view of rewards
goal
goal structure
group cohesion
group goal
hidden agenda
individualistic efforts
inducibility
level of aspiration
merit system
need system
openness
operational goals
psychological health
self-fulfilling prophecy
sharing
social dependence
social interdependence
substitutability
survey-feedback method
trusting behavior
trustworthy behavior

Chapter 4

Objectives:

The following concepts should be understood when this chapter is completed:

interpersonal communication
effective communication
sender
receiver
message
channel
defensive behavior

one-way communication
two-way communication
communication network
information gatekeepers
leveling
sharpening
assimilation

Summary:

Communication is the basis of human interaction and group functioning. A group's existence depends on how well its members communicate. Members must be able to send and receive messages effectively if the group is to be successful. Groups that are focused on problem solving must be comprised of effective communicators who can state positions and listen to other points of view. If a hierarchy exists within the group, a communication network should be established and understood by all group members. Communication networks may be formal or informal, depending on the goals of the group. Environment, such as seating arrangement, room-size, and acoustics, also impacts the effectiveness of group performance.

Activities:

4.1 Your Communication Behavior
4.2 Bewise College
4.3 Solstice-Shenanigans Mystery
4.4 Liepz and Bounz
4.5 Transmission and Information
4.6 One- and Two-Way Communication
4.7 Group Observation
4.8 Norms and Communication
4.9 Sitting in a Circle
4.10 Communication Networks
4.11 Your Communication Behavior

Short-Answer Essay Questions:

1) How does interpersonal communication affect group performance?

2) Define effective communication.

3) Explain the following communication roles: sender, receiver?

4) Define defensive behavior as it relates to group communication.

5) What is one-way communication as it relates to group communication? Provide an example.

6) How is a good communication network within a group structured?

7) What is leveling as it relates to group communication?

8) Why are some groups hierarchical and others not?

9) What is sharpening as it relates to group communication?

10) What is assimilation as it relates to group communication?

Multiple choice:

1) Interpersonal communication is intended to
a)   influence others' behavior.*
b)   make the session interesting.
c)   destroy preconceived thought.
d)   help the facilitator.

2) A message is a
a)   sometimes necessary outcome of interpersonal
        communication.

b)   transmission of a verbal or non-verbal signal.*

c)   both a and b.

d)   none of the above.

3) A creative group solution can occur only when

a)   all necessary information is discussed.

b)   everyone has the chance to speak.

c)   the facilitator gets involved.

d)   a and b.*

4) Defensive behavior occurs in a group when

a)   group members speak loudly.

b)   one person in the group feels threatened.*

c)   a group member leaves unexpectedly.

d)   both a and b.

5) Information acquisition among group members is usually determined by

a)   the communication network.*

b)   the facilitator.

c)   the sender.

d)   the receiver.

6) Appropriate group member behavior is also referred to as

a)   a network.

b)   a norm.*

c)   an art.

d)   a science.

7) A group that is organized

a)   meets regularly.

b)   depends heavily on the facilitator.

c)   follows a consistent pattern of information exchange.

d)   submits a written report after each session.

8) The process of receiving a message and encoding it into one's frame of reference is

a)   accommodation.

b)   assimilation.*

c)   controversy.

d)   feedback.

9) Information and opinion gatekeepers are

a)   clinicians.

b)   pollsters.

c)   moderators.

d)   opinion leaders.*

10) When a receiver minimizes information into one's frame of reference, _____ occurs.

a)   assimilation

b)   accommodation

c)   leveling

d)   controversy

Terms:

assimilation
channel
communication network
defensive behavior
effective communication
information gatekeepers
interpersonal communication
leveling
message
noise
one-way communication
receiver
seating arrangements
sender
sharpening
two-way communication

Chapter 5

Objectives:

The following concepts should be understood once this chapter is completed:

trait approach to leadership	Task actions
charismatic leadership	Relationship actions
Machiavellian leadership	Member maturity
Leadership styles	Telling
Initiating structure	Selling
Influence Leadership	Participating
Role-position approach to leadership	Delegating
Distributed-actions approach to leadership	

Summary

Leadership has a direct impact on overall group functioning and success. Members assume different roles as they relate to leadership. Some members may be more vocal, while others may try to lead through other forms of influence. Regardless, various factors affect the leadership components of a group. Social Determinism requires understanding of social forces, movements, and values which may impact group members' leadership behavior. Charisma among group members also impacts who takes specific roles. The structure of the group, and how its communication network is established helps determine various leadership factors as well.

Activities:
5.1 The Nature of Leadership
5.2 Our Ideal Leaders
5.3 Interpersonal Patterns
5.4 Your Leadership Actions Exercises 1 and 2
5.5 The Least Preferred Co-worker Scale
5.6 How Do You Explain This Leader?
5.7 The Furniture Factory
5.8 Tower Building

Short-Answer Essay Questions:

1) What is the trait approach to leadership?

2) What is charismatic leadership?

3) What is Machiavellian leadership?

4) How can different leadership styles impact a group?

5) Describe the concept of role approach as it pertains to leadership.

6) What are task actions?

7) How does member maturity affect the leadership styles for group dynamics?

8) Explain the correlation between relationship actions and effective leadership.

9) Describe an effective leadership style.

10) Why is delegating important as it pertains to leadership?

Multiple Choice:

1) What is the term for the traditional concept of leadership?
a)   sole proprietorship
b)   lone ranger*
c)   cooperation
d)   assimilation

2) Social Determinism concerns
a)   the impact of social forces on history.
b)   the role society plays in group effectiveness.*
c)   the impact of society on facilitation of a group.
d)   the evolution of society in small group dynamics.

3) Charisma is
a)   intangible.*
b)   earned.
c)   developed.
d)   all of the above.

4) The principle of Machiavellian leadership states that people
a) require a great deal of support.
b) make good leaders.
c) are basically weak.*
d) are insignificant.

5) The influence approach to leadership focuses on
a) reciprocation.
b) susceptibility.*
c) one-way communication.
d) sharpening.

6) Roles are
a) related to expected behaviors within a group.*
b) helpful in determining leadership candidates.
c) convenient for the facilitator.
d) all of the above.

7) Task behavior relates to
a) one-way communication.*
b) two-way communication.
c) social determinism.
d) assimilation.

8) Process observation in a group is concerned with
a) the topic of discussion.
b) how the group interacts with other groups.
c) how group members of the same group interact.*
d) all of the above.

9) The perception of common linkage for common success is known as
a) individual accountability.
b) positive interdependence.*
c) self-efficacy.
d) group processing.

10) Cooperation involves
a) teaming.*
b) working side-by-side on individual projects.
c) self-attribution.
d) group members competing with each other.

Terms:

analysis
charismatic leadership
delegating
distributed-actions approach to leadership
influence Leadership
initiating structure
leadership

leadership styles
Machiavellian leadership
Member maturity
Participating
Relationship actions
Role-position approach to leadership
Selling
Task actions
trait approach to leadership
zeitgeist

Chapter Six:

Objectives:

In this chapter a number of concepts are defined and discussed. The major ones are listed below:

1. Decision
2. Effective decision
3. Consensus
4. Majority vote
5. Minority control
6. Averaging opinions

7. Defensive avoidance
8. Group-think
9. Dissonance reduction
10. Concurrence seeking
11. Critical evaluation
12. Vigilance

Summary

Typically, groups make more effective decisions than do individuals because groups create the possibility for social facilitation, risk taking, member commitment to the group, appropriate behavioral and attitudinal patterns being adopted, and the likelihood that the task is better done in a group. Once a group is given the responsibility for making the decision, there are seven methods to choose from, including letting the member with the highest authority decide to averaging individual opinions to group consensus. In using the decision making methods, there are components that must be carefully structured (positive interdependence, promotive interaction, individual accountability, social skills, and group processing) and there are factors that hinder the group's decision-making efforts. The hindering factors include the lack of group maturity, taking the dominant response, social loafing, free riding, fear of being a sucker, groupthink, conflicting goals, members' egocentrism, homogeneity, production blocking, inappropriate size, dissonance reduction, and the lack of necessary taskwork and teamwork skills. In order to structure the essential components and avoid the hindering factors, the group has to engage in considered and thoughtful decision making. The steps for doing so are to identify and define the problem, gather the information needed to diagnose it, formulate alternative solutions, decide on the solution to implement, present the group's recommendations to the larger organization (if appropriate), and evaluate the success of the implementation to determine if the problem is now solved.

An essential aspect of decision making is deciding among alternative solutions. To do so effectively, conflict among members' preferences, analyses, conclusions, and theories must be encouraged and resolved constructively.

Activities:

6.1 Individual Versus Group Decision Making
6.2 The Bean Jar (I)
6.3 Winter Survival
6.4 They'll Never Take Us Alive
6.5 A Problem Diagnosis Program

6.6 The Bean Jar (II)

6.7 Your Decision-Making Behavior

Short-Answer Essay Questions:

1) What is a decision as it relates to a group?

2) What are the components of an effective decision for a group?

3) What is the difference between the components of an individually-made decision and a good group decision?

4) What are the different methods of achieving a group decision?

5) What are factors which influence group decision making?

6) What is concurrence-seeking in a group?

7) What is vigilance?

8) What is the impact of groupthink on a group's decision?

9) How important is it for all group members to agree on a group decision? Why?

10) Which is the easier: making an individual decision or making a group decision? Why?

Multiple Choice:

1) Assessment of members' contribution to group decision making is called

a) positive interdependence.
b) individual accountability.*
c) group processing.
d) social skill development.

2) Encouragement to achieve among group members is called
a) promotive interaction.*
b) competition.
c) cooperation.
d) a and c.*

3) An identifiable sequence which occurs over time is
a) an event.
b) a pilot project.
c) positive interdependence.
d) a process.*

4) The sequence of events necessary to achieve group goals is called
a) dissonance goals.
b) constructive achievement goals.
c) process goals.*
d) assimilation goals.

5) Which of the following is a hindering factor in group decision making:
a)   positive interdependence.
b)   dominant response.*
c)   group processing.
d)   both b and c.

6) Which of the following is not one of the criteria for making an effective decision:
a)   Time is well used.
b)   The decision is of high quality.
c)   All group members fully implement the decision.
d)   None of the above.*

7) In group decision making, concurrence-seeking refers to
a)   one side giving in to the other's argument.
b)   one side promoting its point of view.
c)   the group coming to a quick decision.*
d)   all sides agreeing to disagree.

8) Which of the following is not a reason why group decision-making may be better than individual decision making?
a)   Higher motivation to achieve.
b)   Increased member commitment.
c)   Cost-effectiveness.*
d)   None of the above.

9) Total group member involvement in the decision-making process will likely result in
a)   a better decision.
b)   increased allegiance to the group.
c)   stronger commitment to future group activities from all
      members.
d)   all of the above.*

10) Decisions should be made by one group member when;
a)   group members are extremely dissimilar.
b)   never, all group members should be involved at all times.
c)   time does not allow for a total group decision and to not
      make a decision would be destructive to the group.*
d)   both a and c.

Terms:

additive task
averaging opinions
concurrence-seeking
consensus
critical evaluation
decision
defensive avoidance
discretionary task
disjunctive task
dissonance reduction

effective decision
expert decision
force-field analysis
free ride
group polarization
group productivity
groupthink
majority vote
minority control
problem
social facilitation
social loafing
sucker effect
vigilance

Chapter Seven

Objectives:

In this chapter a number of concepts are defined and discussed. The major ones are listed below.

1. Controversy
2. Conceptual conflict
3. Epistemic curiosity
4. Cognitive perspective
5. Perspective-taking
6. Concurrence Seeking
7. Debate

8. Creativity
9. Dogmatism
10. Open-mindedness
11. Differentiation of positions
12. Integration of positions
11. Brainstorming

Summary

Decision making typically involves considering possible alternatives and choosing one. By definition, all decision-making situations involve some conflict as to which of several alternatives should be chosen. Within decision-making groups that conflict takes the form of controversy. Controversy exists when one individual's ideas, information, conclusions, theories, and opinions are incompatible with those of another, and the two seek to reach an agreement. Such intellectual conflict among individuals may be avoided and suppressed or it may be structured and encouraged. Simply by emphasizing concurrence-seeking, intellectual conflict among group members may be avoided. And if it does occur, it may be suppressed by stating that it is against the rules.

Most intellectual conflicts are avoided and suppressed. Yet there is evidence that controversy can be a powerful tool. Conflicts among ideas, conclusions, theories, information, perspectives, opinions, and preferences are inevitable. Such conflicts are (a) an inherent aspect of decision making, problem solving, reasoned judgment, and critical thinking, and (b) inevitable. If individuals get intellectually and emotionally involved in cooperative efforts, controversies will occur no matter what participants do. They are critical events that may bring (a) increased learning, creative insight, high quality problem solving and decision making, (b) closer and more positive relationships, and (c) greater social competence and psychological health. Or they may bring closed minds and poorly conceived decisions, lasting resentment and smoldering hostility, and psychological scars, rigidly ineffectual behavior, and a refusal to change or learn.

Controversy begins when your group, faced with a decision that has to be made, assigns the major alternatives to advocacy subgroups and has each subgroup (a) develop its alternative in depth and (b) plan how to present the best case possible for its alternative to the rest of the group. First, group members prepare a position to present to the rest of the group based on their current information, experiences, and perspective. Second, they then present and advocate your position to the rest of the group who, in turn, are advocating opposing positions. High quality decisions and conclusions are reached through a process of argument and counter-argument aimed at persuading others to adopt, modify, or drop positions. Third, group members are confronted by other group members with different positions based on their information, experiences, and perspectives. Members attempt to refute opposing positions while rebutting the attacks on their position. Fourth, faced with these opposing positions, criticisms of your position, and information that is incompatible with and does not fit with their conclusions, they become uncertain as to the correctness of your views. A state of conceptual conflict or disequilibrium is aroused. Group members experience conceptual conflict and uncertainty when faced with (a) opposing positions with their rationales and (b) challenges to the validity of their own position and its rationale. Being challenged by conclusions and information that are incompatible with and do not fit with their reasoning and conclusions results in conceptual conflict, uncertainty, and disequilibrium. Fifth, members' uncertainty, conceptual conflict, and disequilibrium motivates an active search for more information, new experiences, and a more adequate cognitive perspective and reasoning in hopes of resolving the uncertainty. Epistemic curiosity, divergent attention and thought are stimulated. Members search for more information and experiences to support your position, seek to understand opposition positions and rationales, seek to understand the opposing positions and their supporting rationale, and attempt to view the problem from opposing perspectives. This results in a reorganization and reconceptualization of their conclusions. Finally, members adapt their cognitive perspective and reasoning through understanding and accommodating the perspective and reasoning of others and derive a new, reconceptualized, and reorganized conclusion. Novel solutions and decisions that, on balance, are qualitatively better are detected. The purpose of controversy is not to choose the best of the alternatives. The purpose of controversy is to create a synthesis of the best reasoning and conclusions from all the various alternatives. To do so, members have to keep conclusions tentative, accurately understand opposing perspectives, incorporate new information into their conceptual frameworks, and change their attitudes and position. This process is repeated until the differences in conclusions among group members have been resolved, a decision is reached, and the controversy has ended.

Controversies tend to be constructive when the situation context is cooperative, there is some heterogeneity among group members, information and expertise is distributed within the group, members have the necessary conflict skills, and the canons of rational argumentation are followed. An essential aspect of controversy is the creativity that is derived from the collision of adverse opinion.

Activities:
7.1 Controversy
7.2 Your Behavior In Controversies (I)
7.3 Stranded in the Desert
7.4 Who Should Get the Penicillin?
7.5 Fallout Shelter
7.6 The Johnson School
7.7 Avoiding Controversies
7.8 Beliefs About Controversy
7.9 Creativity
7.10 Joe Doodlebug
7.11 Brainstorming
7.12 Creativity Warm-Up
7.13 Your Behavior in Controversies

Short-Answer Essay Questions:

1) What is a controversy as it relates to a group?

2) What is conceptual conflict as it relates to a group?

3) What is epistemic curiosity and how does it impact group decision making?

4) What are the different methods of arguing effectively within a group?

5) What are factors which influence controversy?

6) What is debate?

7) What is creativity as it pertains to group decision making?

8) What is dogmatism?

9) How can a group ensure that all group members agree on a group decision?

10) Which is the better: an individual decision or a group decision? Why?

Multiple Choice:

1) Controversy exists when
a)   two people yell at each other.
b)   one person's ideas are incompatible with another person's ideas.*
c)   all sides agree.
d)   both a and b.

2) In group decision making, advocacy involves
a)   one side giving in to the other's argument.
b)   one side promoting its point of view.*
c)   the group coming to a quick decision.
d)   all sides agreeing to disagree.

3) In group decision making, consensus refers to
a)   one side giving in to the other's argument.
b)   one side promoting its point of view.
c)   the group coming to a quick decision.*
d)   all sides agreeing to disagree.

4) In group decision making, withdrawal refers to
a)   one side giving in to the other's argument.*
b)   one side promoting its point of view.
c)   the group coming to a quick decision.
d)   all sides agreeing to disagree.

5) Total group member involvement in the decision-making process will likely result in
a)   a better decision.
b)   increased allegiance to the group.

c) stronger commitment to future group activities from all members.
d) all of the above.*

6) Decisions should be made by one group member when;
a) group members are extremely dissimilar.
b) never, all group members should be involved at all times.
c) time does not allow for a total group decision and to not make a decision would be destructive to the group.*
d) both a and c.

7) Perspective-taking refers to:
a) one person advocating one perspective.
b) understanding all points of view.
c) listening to the opposing perspective and then advocating it in a structured format.*
d) all of the above.

8) Integration occurs when
a) members arrive at a synthesized decision.*
b) there is diversity within the group.
c) both a and b.
d) none of the above.

9) Groupthink is constructive in decision making when
a) there is very little time.
b) some members are very intimidating.
c) threats exist within the group
d) none of the above.*

10) Which is not an outcome of controversy:
a) productivity.
b) quality.
c) commitment.
d) all of the above.*

Terms:

advocacy
brainstorming
closed belief system
cognitive perspective
conceptual conflict
concurrence-seeking
controversy
creativity
debate
deliberate discourse
differentiation of positions
dogmatism
dualistic thinking
epistemic curiosity

individualistic accountability
integration of positions
open belief system
open-mindedness
perspective-taking
positive interdependence
probablistic thinking
relativistic thinking
skilled disagreement
synthesizing
task involvement

Chapter Eight

Objectives:

In this chapter a number of concepts are defined and discussed. The major ones are listed below:

1. Conflict Positive Group
2. Conflict of interests
3. Withdrawal
4. Forcing
5. Smoothing
6. Compromise
7. Negotiation
8. Distributive, Win-Lose Negotiations
9. Integrative, Problem-Solving Negotiations
10. Goal dilemma
11. Dilemma of trust

12. Dilemma of openness and honesty
13. Norm of reciprocity
14. Steps of integrative negotiating
15. Attribution theory
16. Fundamental attribution error
17. Frustration-aggression process
18. Psychological Reactance
19. Stereotype
20. Self-fulfilling prophecy
21. Superordinate goal
22. Mediation

Summary

If any group is to function effectively, a high level of cooperation among its members must prevail. Whatever the method used to either control or resolve conflicts, it must establish as much cooperation as possible among group members to be effective. The management of conflicts of interests in ways that maximize member cooperation depends on the group having a common set of values and norms about the management of conflict and an agreed-upon vocabulary for discussing conflicts among members.

As with controversies, group members in a conflict of interests must have a system of positive beliefs about fighting: They must view it as a productive way of handling differences. Members must believe that conflicts of interests are natural and should not be avoided or repressed; that the natural tension and frustration of working together can be greatly reduced through conflicts; that conflicts help group members avoid stockpiling anger and resentment and being bothered by the past; and that conflicts bring information to group members about how they are progressing, what is important to each member, and how group work and members' relationships can be improved. In addition to the points on negotiating covered in this chapter, some additional norms and procedures conducive to constructive conflict management are as follows.

1. **The circumstances that brought about the conflict should be understood by group members.** Such circumstances involve both barriers to the beginning of negotiations and events that trigger expressions of the conflict (Walton, 1987). **Internal barriers** include negative attitudes, values, fears, anxieties, and habitual patterns of avoiding conflict. **External barriers** may include task requirements, group norms for avoiding conflict, and faulty perceptions of one's vulnerability and others' strength. Despite these potential barriers, however, particular circumstances called **triggering events** may be capable of bringing about open negotiations. The diagnosis of a conflict involves discovering (a) the barriers to negotiation

and (b) what triggers open expression of the conflict. From such knowledge group members can help choose the time and place for negotiations. If an appropriate time is not immediately available, the barriers to expressing the conflict can be increased and the triggering events can be decreased in order to avoid the conflict temporarily. Some events may trigger a destructive cycle of conflict and others may trigger problem solving; group members will want to maximize the latter type of triggering event. An analysis of events that surround or precede a conflict often provides clues to the basic issues of the conflict.

2. **The entry state of the participants should be assessed by the group.** The **entry state** of a group member is that person's ability to deal constructively with the conflict. Members' level of self-awareness, their ability to control their behavior, their skills in communicating and in other ways being interpersonally effective (see Johnson, 1986), their ability to withstand stress, and their ability to incorporate their strengths in constructive conflict behavior are all important aspects of their entry state. Group support and consultation can raise the entry state of each participant.

3. **Standards and norms should be set on what "weapons" are to be allowed and when "beltlines" are to be established for each member.** The intensity and area of attack should be kept within each member's revealed capacity to deal with the hurt.

4. **The situation power of all participants should be balanced.** Power can involve being more verbal, having a louder voice, or having more authority. The group should help minimize such differences so that negotiations can be conducted among equals.

5. **Intermissions should take place** during which participants can reflect on the conflict and what they are learning from it.

6. **An optimal tension level should be maintained by each throughout the negotiations.** A period of high tension that generates motivation to negotiate in good faith, followed by a reduction to a moderate level of tension that does not interfere with a person's ability to integrate and use information, is often the best way to manage conflicts of interests.

7. The consequences of the conflict of interests should be clearly understood. Consequences can be either costs or gains. When a group is involved in negotiations among its members, an appreciation of the costs and gains of the conflict for each member is essential. Both the primary and the secondary costs and gains for the negotiators and for the group as a whole need to be correctly assessed, especially when members begin using win-lose negotiation strategies. An analysis of the consequences of a conflict may yield an understanding of why the conflict is tending to intensify, subside, or stay at the same pitch. An understanding of the consequences of a conflict permits group members to identify the desirable and realistic ones and plan strategies accordingly. In examining the consequences of a conflict, members should never ignore the positive outcomes; it is all too easy to focus only on the costs and not on the benefits.

8. **The constructive management of conflict often requires a common language about conflicts**. The group language might include such terms as win-lose, problem-solve, confront, beltline, and gunnysack. To gunnysack is to store up grievances for a long time and then unload them all on an offending group member. A common language about conflicts facilitates the identification of constructive and destructive strategies of negotiation. Every group may develop its own vocabulary for describing conflict behaviors and procedures.

9. In negotiations, many participants wish to appear hard to influence. The toughness of negotiators in fighting for their interests is especially important when they are following win-lose strategies and attempting to dominate the opposition. Under such circumstances negotiators may rather not reach a constructive agreement in order to maintain their bargaining reputation. Groups may wish to find ways of minimizing the concern of their members that the reputation of the negotiators will be affected if they reach constructive agreements.

10. Besides being aimed at resolving a conflict, negotiations can have important side effects, such as maintaining contact with an adversary, substituting negotiations for violent action, gathering intelligence, practicing deception, issuing propaganda, and having an impact on third parties (Ikle, 1964). It may be in the interests of the whole group to encourage continued negotiation between two members in order to obtain desired side effects as well as a resolution of the conflict.

11. The most important aspect of negotiating conflicts among group members is to ensure that they focus on the long-term joint outcomes of an agreement, not on short-term individual outcomes. Many conflicts of interests can be resolved in ways that maximize the long-term benefit of the members and the group as a whole. Members who become locked into a win-lose negotiating strategy often focus on short-term self-interests in a way that blinds them to the longer-term mutual benefits to themselves and the entire group. The group should ensure that conflicts of members are resolved so as to maximize secondary rather than primary gains.

Negotiation Strategies: Constructive And Destructive

In the research and theorizing on negotiations, numerous strategies have been suggested. Those in the partial list below were taken from studies of union-management and international negotiations. Because most such negotiations are treated as win-lose situations, the strategies listed are not necessarily recommended by the authors. Readers interested in further study of negotiation strategies, however, are referred to Douglas (1962), Ikle (1964), Schelling (1960), and Stevens (1963).

Every negotiator is continually faced with the threefold choice: (1) accept the available terms for agreement, (2) try to improve the available terms through further negotiation, and (3) discontinue negotiations without agreement and with no intention of resuming them. If the choice is to continue negotiations, a variety of strategies can be used to influence: (1) the opponent's expectations as to what a reasonable outcome is for her, (2) the opponent's perceptions of what one's expectations of a reasonable agreement are, and (3) the opponent's perceptions of how influenceable one is. Among these strategies are the following:

1. Establish the negotiating range or the boundaries of negotiation by adopting an extreme opening offer and refusing to compromise in order to build a reputation of toughness and to influence the opponent's notion of what an acceptable agreement is.
2. Search for possible points of agreement beneath the surface of the current disagreement. Obtaining accurate information about potential agreements that would be acceptable to the opponent is a vital element of their strategy
3. Add new demands until the other negotiator agrees to terms less favorable than those originally proposed.
4. Propose a package deal in which several issues that are considered part of the agreement are settled.
5. Introduce an issue considered extraneous by your opponent - a tie-in - and offer to accept a certain settlement provided this issue is also settled to your satisfaction.
6. Carve an issue out of a larger context, settle it, and leave the related issues unsettled.
7. Coercion: make a threat that you will carry out if the opponent does not agree to your terms.
8. Commit yourself to an action that leaves the last clear chance of avoiding disaster or nonagreement to the other negotiator, thereby limiting her alternatives
9. Create an impression of being uncertain about what you will do, being out of control, or being irrational,
so that the opponent will want to settle quickly before you do serious harm to everyone involved.

Activities:
8.1 Your Conflict Strategies
8.2 Making a Profit
8.3 Group Member Excellence
8.4 Negotiating Resolutions to Conflicts of Interests
8.5 Negotiating Within an Organization
8.6 Breaking Balloons
8.7 Intergroup Conflict
8.8 Artillery Salvos
8.9 Other Intergroup Conflict Exercises
8.10 Intergroup Confrontation (I)
8.11 Intergroup Confrontation (II)
8.12 Your Conflict Behavior

Short-Answer Essay Questions:

1) What is a conflict?

2) What are the strategies for resolving conflicts within a group?

3) What are the steps necessary to achieve a fully negotiated resolution to a conflict?

4) Describe a distributive, win-lose negotiation. What are some of the behaviors that would be exhibited by group members?

5) Describe the importance of trust in negotiating a resolution to a conflict.

6) What is meant by reciprocity and how is it important in resolving group conflicts?

7) What is a stereotype and how does it impact resolution to group conflicts.

8) What is prejudice and how does it impact resolution to group conflicts?

9) What is the difference between mediation and arbitration?

10) What is a self-fulfilling prophecy? What role does it play in resolving in-group conflicts?

Multiple Choice:

1) A conflict within a group exists when
a)   two people agree almost immediately.
b)   at least two people believe their respective position is best.*
c)   at least three people believe their respective position is best.
d)   none of the above.

2) Forcing occurs in a conflict negotiation when
a)   one side attempts to force their will over the others.*
b)   the facilitator takes control of the group.
c)   both a and b.
d)   neither a or b.

3) Compromise usually occurs instead of negotiation when
a)   nobody wants to discuss the issue any longer.
b)   time is in short supply.*
c)   bonus points are given for compromise.
d)   none of the above.

4) A fully negotiated conflict involves
a)   a mediator.
b)   a commitment to honor the agreement from all sides.*
c)   one side winning for its position.
d)   one side giving in.

5) Something which causes a conflict within a group is called
a) a triggering event.*
b) a conflict commencement.
c) trialization.
d) declaration.

6) Equal benefit or cost in conflict negotiation is called
a) exacting.
b) storming.
c) norm of reciprocity.
d) norm of equity.*

7) When negotiators depend on each other, they are considered to be
a) partners.
b) teammates.
c) interdependent.
d) all of the above.*

8) Return of harm or benefit is called the
a) eye/tooth principle.
b) norm of equity principle.
c) norm of reciprocity principle.*
d) none of the above.

9) A guiltless defenseless group member can be considered a
a) patsy.
b) victim.
c) normative target.
d) scapegoat.*

10) Two youth groups have a history of intergroup conflict. Which of the following would be the best way to resolve this conflict:
a) Build a gymnasium which both groups may use.
b) Hold a basketball tournament in which both groups may participate.
c) Have both groups work together to sponsor a car wash.*
d) none of the above.

Terms:

attribution theory
compromise
conflict-positive group
conflicts of interests
contractual norms
dilemma of openness
dilemma of trust
distributive negotiation
forcing
frustration-aggression process
fully negotiated conflict resolution
fundamental attribution error
goal

goal dilemma
information dependence
mediation
need
negotiation
norm of reciprocity
persuasive argument
preemptive actionsocial perspective-taking
psychological reactance
self-fulfilling prophecy
smoothing
stereotype
superordinate goal
triggering event
want
withdrawal

Chapter Nine

Objectives:

In this chapter a number of concepts are defined and discussed. The major ones are listed below.

1. Trait-factor view of power
2. Dynamic-interdependence view of power
3. Credibility
4. Attractiveness
5. Forewarning
6. Innovation
7. Power
8. Outcome dependence
9. Information dependence
10. Resistance
11. Manipulation
12. Rule of self-direction
13. Reward Power
14. Legitimate power
15. Referent power
16. Information power
17. Expert power
18. Coercion power

Summary

Attempts to exert power over other group members are enhanced if one is credible and attractive; if one phrases one's messages so that they are two sided, action oriented, and discrepant with members' current beliefs; and if the other group members have low self-esteem, see their attitudes under modification as peripheral to them, have no forewarning of the influence attempt, role play positions that agree with one's own, have not been inoculated, are distracted while one is presenting the message, and are not very intelligent. The trait-factor approach to influence, however, is weak both logically and empirically in situations where two or more individuals are constantly interacting. We thus turn next to the dynamic-interdependence approach to influence.

The trait-factor approach to influence views power as an attribute of a person. A person exerts power by (a) being credible and attractive, (b) phrasing messages so that they are two sided, action oriented, and discrepant with members' current beliefs, and (c) playing on others' low self-esteem and low intelligence, giving them no forewarning of the influence attempt, distracting them during the influence attempt, convincing them the attitudes under modification are peripheral to them, and having them role play positions counter to their beliefs.

The dynamic-interdependence approach to influence views power as an attribute of an interpersonal relationship. In a relationship people are dependent on each other for outcomes and information. There is an aversion to being controlled and, therefore, the direct use of power in a relationship has to be done carefully. The base of the use of power may make a difference. Power may be based on the ability to deliver rewards, the ability to deliver punishments, a position of authority, being a referent for others, being an expert, and having needed information. When the distribution of power is unequal, both the high- and low-power person have problems. While the use of person is ever present in a relationship, it is during conflicts that individuals become most conscious of its use.

Finally, besides the direct use of power, there are indirect ways to exert influence. The primary way is through group norms. When group members conform to the normative expectations they are being influenced. Most power is exerted through indirect means such as group norms. The mass hysteria and panic that is sometimes observed in groups may have its origins in the groupmind, converging with people who share similar convictions and predisposition's, following norms that emerge in the group, or members' becoming deindividualized. Being influenced by the group is not all bad. The group can encourage members to behave altruistically.

Activities:
9.1 Power Origin
9.2 Personal Power and Personal Goal Accomplishment
9.3 Unequal Resources
9.4 Power Politics
9.5 Power to the Animals
9.6 Summer Campers
9.7 Group Power
9.8 Developing Land Areas

Short-Answer Essay Questions:

1) What is power?

2) How is power within a group determined?

3) What is unequal power?

4) How does power within a group affect conflict negotiations?

5) What is referent power?

6) What is legitimate power?

7) What is reward power?

8) What is resistance?

9) What is manipulation?

10) Explain the difference between outcome dependence and information dependence.

Multiple Choice:

1) When the group leader controls both positive and negative consequences, there exists
a)	legitimate power.
b)	referent power.
c)	information power.
d)	coercive power.*

2) When only the group leader has resources which are useful in accomplishing the goal, there exists
a)   legitimate power.
b)   referent power.
c)   information power.*
d)   coercive power.

3) When group members believe that the group leader should have authority because of special role responsibilities, there exists
a)   legitimate power.
b)   referent power.*
c)   information power.
d)   coercive power.

4) Power which is based on group members identification with or attraction to the power holder is known as
a)   legitimate power.
b)   referent power.*
c)   information power.
d)   coercive power.

5) When group members agree to commit to an agreement before negotiations commence, there exists
a)   information dependence.
b)   outcome dependence.*
c)   forced settlement.
d)   outcome interdependence.

6) When goals and rewards directing individuals actions are positively correlated, or when one person accomplishes his or her goal and all others within the group are linked to that accomplishment, there exists
a)   information dependence.
b)   outcome dependence.
c)   forced settlement.
d)   outcome interdependence. *

7) Power and influence in a group should be based on
a)   ability.
b)   expertise.
c)   information access.
d)   all of the above.*

8) Group influences which change behavior produce
a)   compliance.
b)   conformity.*
c)   response.
d)   power.

9) A shrewd management of others is called
a)   power.
b)   coerciveness.
c)   manipulation.*
d)   legitimate power.

10) The attempt to change group member behavior is called
a)   attractiveness.

b) power.

c) influence.*

d) none of the above.

Terms:

attractiveness
coercion power
control
credibility
deindividuation
expert power
forewarning
high power
influence
information dependence
information power
innovation
legitimate power
low power
manipulation
outcome dependence
power
referent power
resistance
reward power
rule of self-direction
trait-factor view of power
unequal power

Chapter Ten

Objectives:
In this chapter a number of concepts are defined and discussed. The major ones are listed below

1. Demographic diversity
2. Personal diversity
3. Ability and skill diversity
4. Group composition
5. Intellective tasks

6. Performance tasks
7. Decision-making tasks
8. Personal identity
9. Superordinate group identity
10. Language sensitivity

Summary

In a global village highly diverse individuals interact daily, studying, working, and playing together in small groups. Rapidly growing global interdependence and the increasing emphasis on teamwork results in groups with quite diverse membership. Diversity among members is no longer the exception, or optional, it is the everyday rule. Global interdependence and diversity among team members go hand-in-hand. With the one, comes the other. Diversity among your acquaintances, classmates, coworkers, neighbors, and friends is increasingly inevitable. You will be expected to interact effectively with people from a wide variety of characteristics and backgrounds. Doing so has many advantages. Heterogeneity of group composition tends to increase group productivity on a variety of tasks, increase the difficulty for developing cohesive relationships among members, and increases the potential conflict among members. Diversity among members is advantageous, but it is not easy to manage.

Accepting others begins with accepting yourself .But even for individuals who are quite accepting of themselves and others, there are barriers to building positive relationships with diverse peers. The most notable barriers are prejudice, blaming the victim, and culture clash. Minimizing these barriers makes it easier to recognize that diversity exists and fundamental differences among people are to be both respected and valued. For group members to capitalize on their differences, they must ensure high levels of positive interdependence exist among group members (highlight important mutual goals that require cooperative action and develop a common ground on which everyone is cooriented), create a superordinate group identity that (a) unites the diverse personal identities of group members and (b) is based on a pluralistic set of values, gain sophistication about the differences among members through personal relationships that have sufficient trust to allow for candid discussions, and clarify miscommunications that arise when group members from different cultures, ethnic and historical backgrounds, social classes, genders, age-cohorts, and so forth, work together.

Activities:
10.1 Greetings and Good-byes
10.2 Time
10.3 Cross-Cultural Communication
10.4 Merging Different Cultures

Short-Answer Essay Questions:

1) What is demographic diversity?

2) How does group diversity differ from personal diversity?

3) What is ability diversity?

4) What is the ideal demographic composition of a group. Why?

5) How is personal identity formed?

6) What is meant by superordinate group identity?

7) Explain the importance of language sensitivity in group functioning.

8) How does language impact group functioning?

9) How is time a function of diversity within a group?

10) What are performance tasks? How do they impact group productivity?

1) Which of the following statements is true?
a)   Our society is changing in its make-up.
b)   Understanding of all cultures is necessary if one is to lead
     groups effectively.
c)   The world order is evolving.
d)   All of the above.*

2) One source of diversity in group member personal characteristics is
a) democratic differences.
b) personality differences.*
c) liking differences.
d) none of the above.

3) Which of the following statements is true?
a) Group members must be somewhat similar if good work is to be done.
b) Similar demographics among group members often lead to quicker decisions.
c) Group members can have different personalities and learning styles.*
d) All of the above.

4) Performance tasks
a) deal strictly with execution of a group assignment.
b) help weed-out social loafers.
c) require the proficient use of perceptual and motor skills to be productive.
d) all of the above.*

5) Intellective tasks
a) are done on an optional basis.
b) focus on solving problems with correct answers.*
c) neither a or b.
d) both a and b.

6) Decision-making tasks
a) deal with finding a solution that is already known.
b) are often very difficult.
c) are problem solving tasks with correct answers.
d) involve reaching a consensus about the best solution to a problem which is not already known.*

7) Ability composition of groups
a) affects overall group performance.
b) is not always feasible.
c) is often preferred by relatives of high achievers.
d) all of the above.*

8) Which of the following statements is true?
a) It's easy to assign group membership.
b) Groups can be assigned in any fashion to fit any task.
c) It is difficult to determine important attributes when assigning group membership.*
d) None of the above.

9) Blaming the victim occurs when

a) the personal characteristics of the victim are cited as the reasons for misfortune.*

b) there is no other apparent reason for misfortune.

c) the perpetrator of misfortune cannot be determined.

d) none of the above.

10) Discrimination is an action

a) that occurs only to minorities.

b) that is never present in group functioning.

c) taken to harm a group or any of its members.*

d) none of the above.

Terms:

ability diversity
blaming the victim
culture clash
decision-making tasks
demographic diversity
discrimination
diversity
ethnocentrism
false consensus bias
group composition
illusionary correlation
intellective tasks
language sensitivity
performance tasks
personal diversity
personal identity
prejudice
superordinate group identity

Chapters 11 and 12

Objectives:
The following concepts should be understood upon completion of these chapters:

1. The nature of learning groups
2. The stages of development for learning groups
3. Basic procedures for structuring discussion groups.
4. Changing ownership from coordinator to group members.
5. The coordinator's role.
6. Events that promote participant change.
7. Establishing the goals of a growth group.
8. Leading a growth group.
9. Becoming a facilitator. How growth groups affect participant anxiety.

Summary
The coordinator of a discussion group must introduce, define, and structure the learning and growth group. The coordinator should also clarify procedures, reinforce members for conforming to the procedures, and help members become acquainted. The coordinator should also emphasize and highlight

the cooperative interdependence among group members and encourage engaging in trusting behaviors as well as accept rebellion by and differentiation among group members. Although all group members are responsible for behaving in ways that help one another learn, the coordinator may be more qualified than most other members to facilitate helpful behaviors. The coordinator may also serve as gatekeeper of the physical structure of the group. This concern includes offering a summary at the end of each group session.

Short-Answer Essay Questions:

1) How should a coordinator develop procedures that will promote maximum group performance?

2) What are the stages of development for learning groups?

3) How does an effective transition from coordinator to group members occur?

4) How should discussion groups be structured?

5) What is the most effective method for coordinating discussion groups?

6) What is a growth group?

7) Describe self-actualization and its role in group functioning.

8) How are relationships humanized by the coordinator in group functioning?

9) What is reactance?

10) Why is conceptual framework important in structuring a group?

1) A group whose primary purpose is to learn is called
a)   a discussion group.
b)   a learning group.*
c)   an intellectual group.
d)   none of the above.

2) Group cohesiveness is established during which of the following stages:
a)   forming
b)   norming*
c)   fermenting
d)   following

3) When a group experience finishes, the coordinator should help provide
a)   termination.
b)   finalizing.
c)   closure.*
d)   decompression.

4) Room design (is)
a)   not relevant to group performance.
b)   indicates what is expected from the group experience.*
c)   determined by the coordinator.
d)   none of the above.

5) One way to arrange cooperative interdependence is to
a)   assign roles.*
b)   let members choose roles.
c)   provide a simple task which any member can do alone.
d)   none of the above.

6) Learning group quality should be evaluated
a)   on-site.*
b)   by an outside researcher who visits periodically.
c)   by a learning group specialist who telephones the coordinator.
d)   none of the above.

7) Group processing in a learning group is effective for
a)   venting.
b)   evaluation.
c)   individual accountability.
d)   all of the above.*

8) Coordinators are usually
a)   more qualified. *
b)   less qualified.
c)   trained professionals in the field.
d)   none of the above.

9) During group discussion, the coordinator should help
a)   establish norms for group members.
b)   offer insights when appropriate.
c)   maintain an atmosphere conducive to discussion.
d)   all of the above.*

10) Growth groups assist in the development of
a)   member hostility.
b)   member maturity.*
c)   outcome dependence.
d)   all of the above.

Terms:

differentiation
growth group
interpersonal effectiveness
intervention
mutuality
participant anxiety

reactance
rebellion
self-actualization
terminating
trust

Chapter 13:

Objectives;

In this chapter a number of concepts are defined and discussed. The major ones are listed below.

1. Mass-production organizational structure
2. High-performance organizational structure
3. Organizational development
4. Team training
5. Pareto chart
6. Total quality management

Summary

A **team** is a set of interpersonal interactions structured to achieve established goals. Teams may be differentiated from small groups and from working groups. A team's performance includes team work products that require the joint efforts of two or more members as well as individual work products. Teams may be classified in a number of ways, such as by the setting in which they are used (work, sports, learning), their use in an organization (problem solving, special purpose, self-managing), or what they do (recommend, make or do something, run things). Through the use of modern electronics (such as electronic mail, bulletin boards, and computer conferences), teams can consist of individuals who are widely separated geographically. Teams exist within organizational contexts that greater influence their effectiveness by presenting opportunities and constraints. A general estimate is that more than 85 percent of the behavior of members of an organization is directly attributable to the organization's structure, not the nature of the individuals involved There are basically two organizational contexts--a mass-production organizational structure or a team-based, high-performance organizational structure. The team-based organizational structure is considered to be the wave of the future because of the relationship between teams and productivity. A number of recent meta-analyses have all found that under a wide range of conditions teams are more effective than having individuals work by themselves. The productivity of teams is not a simple function of team members' technical competencies and task abilities. To be productive, teams (like all groups) must ensure members perceive strong positive interdependence, interact in ways that promote each other's success and well-being, be individually accountable, employ their small team skills, and process how effectively the team has been working.

If high quality products and services are to be created, organizations are well advised to use teams. Teams are the basic unit of performance for most organizations. Teams need to be formed, carefully structured to be effective, and nurtured. Nurturing teams includes training and retraining members on both taskwork and teamwork skills as well as engaging in team-building procedures to ensure that their effectiveness keeps improving. The point of carefully structuring teams, training team members, and building team effectiveness is to deliver high quality products and services to customers. Implementing total-quality management procedures involves focusing on the process by which work gets done rather than on inspecting the finished product or service. Teams have to be able to draw flow charts of the way they work and measure their productiveness. Finally, despite how carefully teams are formed and developed, there are problem behaviors that must be dealt with. Through progressively refining procedures and continuous improvement of members' teamwork skills and the team's procedures, the problems can be solved.

Short-Answer Essay Questions:

1) What is a <u>team</u>?

2) What are different types of teams?

3) How does the <u>organizational context</u> in which teams work shape member behavior?

4) What is <u>organizational development</u>?

5) What is <u>organizational effectiveness</u>?

6) Explain three steps to <u>organizational diagnosis</u>.

7) How are productive teams built?

8) What does the research say about team effectiveness? Cite examples.

9) What are three issues which must be considered when forming teams?

10) How is team commitment built?

1) A team is
a)   a group of loosely connected group members.
b)   a set of interpersonal interactions structured to achieve goals.*
c)   both a and b.
d)   neither a or b.

2) Work teams are structured to
a)   put people to work.
b)   maximize member success in doing their jobs.*
c)   both a and b.
d)   neither a or b.

3) sports teams are structured to
a)   help members better their individual performance.
b)   integrate members efforts with those of other team members.
c)   both a and b.*
d)   neither a or b.

4) Problem-solving teams are
a)   structured to help individual performance.
b)   structured to integrate members efforts with those of other members.
c)   off-line discussion groups which have little formal power.*
d)   none of the above.

5) Special-purpose teams are teams which
a)   help all organization members learn.
b)   are limited in structure and scope.
c)   focus on quality and productivity improvements.*
d)   all of the above.

6) Self-managing teams
a)   produce an entire product.
b)   provide an entire service.
c)   both a and b.*
d)   neither a or b.

7) Teams that recommend things
a)   usually last for the life of the organization.
b)   usually have predetermined completion dates.*
c)   both a and b.
d)   neither a or b.

8) Teams that make or do things
a)   are usually very focused.*
b)   usually operate away from the rest of the company.
c)   both a and b.
d)   neither a or b.

9) Teams that run things are
a)   autocratic.
b)   rare, especially in large complex organizations.*
c)   both a and b.
d)   neither a or b.

10) The use of diagnosis and intervention procedures to promote effective
    organizational behavior is called
a)   organization effectiveness.
b)   effective teaming.
c)   organizational development.*
d)   none of the above.

Terms:

cause-and-effect diagram
check sheet
diagnosis
high-performance organizational structure
learning team
mass-production organizational structure
organization effectiveness
organizational context
organizational development
Pareto chart
problem-solving team
scatter diagram
self-managing team
special-purpose team
sports team
team
team building
team training
total quality management

Glossary

Action research: The use of the scientific method in solving research questions that have significant social value.

Action theory: Theory as to what actions are needed to achieve a desired consequence in a given situation.

Additive tasks: Tasks for which group productivity represents the sum of individual member efforts.

Aggregate: Collections of individuals who do not interact with one another.

Arbitration: A form of third-party intervention in negotiations in which recommendations of the person intervening are binding on the parties involved.

Assimilation: Changing a message to fit into your own cognitive frameworks and perspective.

Attribution theory: A social psychological explanation of how individuals make inferences about the causes of behaviors and events.

Authority: Legitimate power vested in a particular position to ensure that individuals in subordinate positions meet the requirements of their organizational role.

Autocratic leader: A leader who dictates orders and determines all policy without involving group members in decision making.

Bargaining: (see negotiations)

Blaming the victim: Attribution of the cause of discrimination or misfortune to the personal characteristics and actions of the victim.

Cathexis: The investment of psychological energy in objects and events outside of oneself.

Cause-and-effect diagram: Visual representation of the relationship between some effect (the problem being studied) and its possible causes.

Channel: The means of sending a message to another person, such as sound and sight.

Charisma: An extraordinary power, as of working miracles.

Charismatic leader: A person who has (1) an extraordinary power or vision and who is able to communicate it to others, or (2) unusual powers of practical leadership that will enable her to achieve the goals that will alleviate followers' distress.

Check sheet: Form to record the frequency with which certain events are happening.

Cognitive dissonance: When a person possesses two cognitions that contradict each other. The theory developed by Leon Festinger predicts that dissonance is uncomfortable and a person will seek to reduce it.

Cognitive structure: A set of principles and processes that organizes cognitive experience.

Cohesiveness: All the forces (both positive and negative) that cause individuals to maintain their membership in specific groups. These include attraction to other group members and a close match between individuals' needs and the goals and activities of the group. The attractiveness that a group has for its members and that the members have for one another.

Communication: A message sent by a person to a receiver(s) with the conscious intent of affecting the receiver's behavior.

Communication networks: Representations of the acceptable paths of communication between persons in a group or organization.

Competitive goal structure: A negative correlation among group members' goal attainments; when group members perceive that they can obtain their goals if and only if the other members with whom they are competitively linked fail to obtain their goal.

Compliance: Behavior in accordance with a direct request. Behavioral change without internal acceptance.

Conflict of interest: When the actions of one person attempting to maximize his or her needs and benefits prevent, block, interfere with, injure, or in some way make less effective the actions of another person attempting to maximize his or her needs and benefits.

Consensus: A collective opinion arrived at by a group of individuals working together under conditions that permit communications to be sufficiently open and the group climate to be sufficiently supportive for everyone in the group to feel that he or she has had a fair chance to influence the decision.

Conformity: Changes in behavior that result from group influences. Yielding to group pressures when no direct request to comply is made.

Construct: A concept, defined in terms of observable events, used by a theory to account for regularities or relationships in data.

Conjunctive tasks: Tasks for which group productivity is determined by the effort or ability of the weakest member.

Concurrence-seeking: Situation where members of a decision- making group inhibit discussion to avoid any disagreement or arguments and emphasize agreement; there is a suppression of different conclusions, an emphasis on quick compromise, and a lack of disagreement within a decision-making group.

Confrontation: The direct expression of one's view of the conflict and one's feelings about it and at the same time an invitation to the opposition to do the same.

Contingency theory of leadership: A theory suggesting that leader effectiveness is determined both by characteristics of leaders and by several situation factors.

Contractual norms that spell out the rules to be observed and the penalties for violating them.

Controversy: The situation that exists when one group member's ideas, information, conclusions, theories, and opinions are incompatible with those of another, and the two seek to reach an agreement.

Cooperative goal structure: A positive correlation among group members' goal attainments; when group members perceive that they can achieve their goal if and only if the other members with whom they are cooperatively linked obtain their goal.

Critical path method: Identifying the final goal and working backward to detail what must happen (tasks and subgoals) before it is achieved, what resources must be allocated, what the timetable for accomplishing each subgoal should be, and who should have what responsibilities.

Culture clash: Conflict over basic values among individuals from different cultures.

Debate: Situation where group members present the best case for positions that are incompatible with one another and a winner is declared on the basis of who presented the best position.

Decision making: Obtaining some agreement among group members as to which of several courses of action is most desirable for achieving the group's goals. The process through which groups identify problems in achieving the group's goals and attain solutions to them.

Decision-making tasks: Tasks that require consensus about the best solution to a problem when the "correct" answer is not known.

Deindividuation: A psychological state characterized by reduced self-awareness and major shifts in perception. It is encouraged by certain eternal conditions (e.g., anonymity) and enhances the performance of wild, impulsive forms of behavior.

Democratic leader: A leader who sets policies through group discussion and decision, encouraging and helping group members to interact, requesting the cooperation of others, and being considerate of members' feelings and needs.

Deutsch, Morton: Social psychologist who theorized about cooperative, competitive, and individualistic goal structures.

Dilemma of honesty and openness: The risk of either being exploited for disclosing too much too quickly or seriously damaging the negotiating relationship by refusing to disclose information and thereby seeming to be deceitful or distrusting.

Dilemma of trust: Choice between believing the other negotiator and risking potential exploitation or disbelieving the other negotiator and risking no agreement.

Discrimination: Action taken to harm a group or any of its members.

Disjunctive tasks: Tasks for which group performance is determined by the most competent or skilled member.

Distributed-actions theory of leadership: The performance of acts that help the group to complete its task and to maintain effective working relationships among its members.

Effective communication: When the receiver interprets the sender's message in the same way the sender intended it.

Egocentrism: Embeddedness in one's own viewpoint to the extent that one is unaware of other points of view and of the limitations of one's perspectives.

Equity or merit view of distributing rewards: Presented by Homans (1961) as a basic rule of distributive justice and equity theory: In a just distribution, rewards will be distributed among individuals in proportion to their contributions. In other words, those members who contribute the most to the group's success should receive the greatest benefits.

Equality system of distributive justice: All group members are distributed equally among group members.

Ethnocentrism: Tendency to regard one's own ethnic group, nation, religion, culture, or gender as being more "correct" than others.

Evaluation apprehension: Concern over being evaluated by others. Such concern may increase arousal and may play an important role in social facilitation.

Experiential learning: Generating an action theory from your own experiences and then continually modifying it to improve your effectiveness.

False consensus bias: A belief (often false) that most other people think and feel very much as we do, such as sharing our stereotypes (such as believing that poor people are lazy).

Field experiment: A study conducted in a natural setting in which the investigator deliberately produces variations in the natural situation in order to examine their effects on group behavior.

FIRO (fundamental interpersonal relations orientation): A theory of interpersonal behavior based on three interpersonal needs: inclusion, control, and affection.

Flow chart: Visual tool to display all steps in a process.

Force field analysis: Portraying the problem as a balance between forces working in opposite directions-- some helping the movement toward the desired state of affairs and others restraining such movement. The balance that results between the helping and restraining forces is the actual state of affairs--a **quasi-stationary equilibrium** that can be altered through changes in the forces.

Frustration-aggression process: Frustration due to the inability to achieve one's goals produces a readiness to respond in an aggressive manner which may boil over into hostility and violence if situation cues that serve as "releasers" are present.

Fundamental attribution error: The attribution of the causes of other's behaviors to personal (disposition) factors and the causes of one's own behavior to situation (environmental) factors. In explaining the causes of the other's behavior the attributer overestimates the causal importance of personality, beliefs, attitudes, and values, and underestimates the causal importance of situation pressures. The opposite is done in explaining the causes of one's own behavior.

Gatekeeper: Person who translates and interprets messages, information, and new developments to groupmates.

Goal: A desired place toward which people are working, a state of affairs that people value.

Goal structure: The type of social interdependence specified among individuals as they strive to achieve their goals.

Great person theory of leadership: A theory suggesting that all great leaders share key traits that equip them for positions of power and authority.

Group: Two or more individuals in face-to-face interaction, each aware of his or her membership in the group, each aware of the others who belong to the group, and each aware of their positive interdependence as they strive to achieve mutual goals.

Group dynamics: The area of social science that focuses on advancing knowledge about the nature of group life. The scientific study of behavior in groups to advance our knowledge about the nature of groups, group development, and the interrelations between groups and individuals, other groups, and larger entities.

Group effectiveness: Success by the group in (1) achieving its goals, (2) maintaining good working relationships among members, and (3) developing and adapting to changing conditions to improve its ability to achieve 1 and 2.

Group efficacy: The expectation of successfully obtaining valued outcomes through the joint efforts of the group members.

Group goal: A future state of affairs desired by enough members of a group to motivate the group to work towards its achievement.

Group influence: The impact of groups on their members.

Group polarization: The tendency of group members to shift toward more extreme positions than those held initially, as a function of group discussion.

Group processing: Reflecting on a group session to (a) describe what member actions were helpful and unhelpful and (b) make decisions about what actions to continue or change.

Group structure: A stable pattern of interaction among group members created by a role structure and group norms.

Groupthink: The tendency of members of highly cohesive groups led by dynamic leaders to adhere to shared views so strongly that they totally ignore external information inconsistent with these views. A mode of thinking in which group members' strivings for unanimity override their motivation to realistically appraise alternative courses of action. A strong concurrence-seeking tendency that interferes with effective group decision making.

Hawthorne effect: A change in behavior that occurs when individuals know they are being observed by researchers.

Hero-traitor dynamic: The negotiator who "wins" is seen as a "hero" and the one who "loses" is perceived to be a "traitor."

Hidden agendas: Personal goals that are unknown to all the other group members and are at cross-purposes with the dominant group goals.

Histogram: Visual representation of frequency of how continuous measurement data are clustered and dispersed across a range of values.

Illusionary correlation: Association perceived between two unrelated factors, such as being poor and being lazy, usually leading to stereotypes.

Independent variable: The variable manipulated by the researcher in an experiment; the causal factor in a cause/effect relationship.

Individual accountability: Assessing the quality and quantity of each member's contributions and giving the results to all group members.

Individuation: Maintaining a sense of unique individual identity.

Individualistic goal structure: No correlation among group members' goal attainments; when group members perceive that obtaining their goal is unrelated to the goal achievement of other members.

Inducibility: Openness to influence.

Information dependence: Dependence on others for information about their preferences, needs, and expectations so that an agreement can be reached.

Influence leader: A person who exerts more influence on other group members than they exert on him.

Intellective tasks: Problem solving tasks with correct answers.

Interest: Need, goal, benefit, profit, advantage, concern, right, or claim.

Integration: Combining several positions into one new, creative position.

Laissez-faire leader: A leader who does not participate in group's decision making at all.

Leader: An individual in a group who exerts the greatest influence on other members.

Leadership: The process through which leaders exert their impact on other group members.

Level of aspiration (LOA): The compromise between ideal goals and more realistic expectations.   A concept developed primarily by Kurt Lewin to explain how people set and revise goals themselves and their groups. Generally, individuals enter situations with an ideal outcome in mind but revise their goals upward after success and downward after failure.

Leveling: Making a message shorter, more concise, and more easily grasped and told. The reciprocal of sharpening.

Lewin, Kurt: Father of group dynamics; social psychologist who originated field theory, experimental group dynamics, and applied group dynamics.

Machiavellian leadership: Leadership based on the beliefs that (1) people are basically weak, fallible, and gullible, and not particularly trustworthy; (2) others are impersonal objects; and (3) one should manipulate others whenever it is necessary in order to achieve one's ends.

Mediation: A form of third-party intervention in negotiations in which a neutral person recommends a nonbinding agreement.

Message: Any verbal or nonverbal symbol that one person transmits to another; the subject matter being referred to in a symbolic way (all words are symbols).

Need distribution of rewards: A situation in which the group members who are most in need of the rewards receive a disproportionate amount of them. A rule suggesting that individuals receive a share of available rewards reflecting their current needs.

Negative monitoring: Monitoring unpleasant, unrewarding, frustrating, destructive, counterproductive behaviors.

Negotiating: A process by which persons who want to come to an agreement try to work out a settlement by exchanging proposals and counterproposals.

Noise: Any element that interferes with the communication process.

Norms: The rules or expectations that specify appropriate behavior in the group; the standards by which group members regulate their actions.

Norm of equity: Norm specifying that the benefits received or the costs assessed by the negotiators should be equal.

Norm of reciprocity: Norm that a negotiator should return the same benefit or harm given him or her by the other negotiator; "an eye for an eye and a kiss for a kiss" is an example of a norm of reciprocity.

Observational research: The systematic description and recording of events that occur in groups by observers.

Operational goals: Goals for which specific steps to achievement are clear and identifiable.

Organizational development: The use of diagnosis and intervention procedures to promote effective interpersonal, group, and intergroup behavior within the organization.

Outcome dependence: Dependence on others to agree to one's proposals in negotiations. Because all parties must commit themselves to an agreement, each is dependent upon the others for the outcome.

Package deal: Several issues being negotiated are all included as part of the agreement.

Pareto chart: Form of vertical bar chart that is used to display the frequency and relative importance of problems, causes, or conditions in order to choose the starting point for process improvement.

Participant observer: A person who is skilled enough to both participate in group work and observe group process at the same time; analysis of the group process and functioning by a participating member of the group.

Performance tasks: Tasks that can only be completed through the proficient use of perceptual and motor skills.

Personal space: The distance that people like to keep between themselves and others.

Perspective taking: Ability to understand how a situation appears to another person and how that person is reacting cognitively and emotionally to the situation.

Prejudice: An unjustified negative attitude toward a person based solely on that individual's membership in a group other than one's own.

Prisoner's dilemma game: Non-zero sum game used by Deutsch and others to investigate trust and conflict.

Primary groups: Small groups characterized by face-to-face interaction, interdependency, and strong group identification such as families and very close friends.

Problem: A discrepancy or difference between an actual state of affairs and a desired state of affairs.

Process consultation: An organizational development procedure of analyzing group functioning by an observing expert.

Process loss: Losses in members' performance due to their participation in the group.

Promise: The statement that if you do as I want, I will engage in an act that will benefit you. A negotiator stating that if the other performs a desired act the negotiator will make sure the other receives benefits.

Psychodynamic fallacy: Seeing the motivation for the other's behavior in terms of personality factors rather than the dynamics of intergroup conflict.

Reactance: People's need to reestablish their freedom whenever it is threatened.

Reference group: A group people identify with, compare their attitudes to, and use as a means to evaluate those attitudes.

Referent power: Power based on the group members' identification with, attraction to, or respect for the powerholder.

Resource attractor: An attribute (such as ability or training) that tends to attract other resources because it gives the possessor an advantage in a competition for these other resources.

Reward power: Power based on the powerholder's control over the positive and negative reinforcements desired by other group members.

Risky-shift: The tendency for individuals to recommend riskier courses of action following group discussion than was true prior to such interaction. The tendency for groups to make riskier decisions than individuals.

Role: A set of expectations defining appropriate behaviors associated with a position within a group. The "part" played by a member of a group. Rules or understandings about the tasks persons occupying certain positions within a group are expected to perform.

Run chart: Line graph used to monitor the behavior of a selected characteristic over time.

Scapegoat: A guiltless but defenseless group who is attacked to provide an outlet for pent-up anger and frustration caused by another group.

Scatter diagram: Displays the cause and effect relationship between two process variables or characteristics.

Self-efficacy: The expectation of successfully obtaining valued outcomes through personal effort; expectation that if one exerts sufficient effort, one will be successful.

Self-fulfilling prophecy: A set of actions that provokes the other into engaging in behavior that confirms one's original assumptions. An example is assuming that the other is belligerent and then proceeding to engage in hostile behavior thereby provoking the other into belligerent actions, which confirms the original assumption.

Sharpening: Selective perceiving and remembering of a few high points of a message while most of the rest is forgotten. The reciprocal of leveling.

Situation approach to leadership: The view that those members of a group most likely to become leaders are those who can best help it to reach its major goals.

Social exchange: A form of social interaction in which participants exchange something of value. What they exchange can range from specific goods or services through information. love, and approval.

Social determinism: The view that historic events are determined by social forces, social movements, and changing social values; see Zeitgeist.

Social facilitation: The enhancement of well-learned responses in the presence of others. Effects on performance resulting from the presence of others.

Social interaction: Patterns of mutual influence linking two or more persons.

Social loafing: A reduction of individual effort when working with others on an additive group task.

Social sensitivity: The ability to perceive and respond to the needs, emotions, and preferences of others.

Social skills training: A structured intervention designed to help participants to improve their interpersonal skills. It is generally conducted in group settings.

Socioemotional activity: Behavior that focuses on interpersonal relations in the group.

Sociometry: A measurement procedure developed by Moreno that is used to summarize graphically and mathematically patterns of interpersonal attraction in groups.

Stereotype: Set of cognitive generalizations that summarize, organize, and guide the processing of information about members of a particular group.

Superordinate goals: Goals that cannot be easily ignored by members of two antagonistic groups, but whose attainment is beyond the resources and efforts of either group alone; the two groups, therefore, must join in a cooperative effort in order to attain the goals.

Superordinate identity: Group identity that transcends the personal, gender, ethnic, and religious identities of group members.

Survey feedback: An organizational development procedure that focuses on describing the current state of the organization through surveys or interviews and then sharing this descriptive information through feedback.

Synthesizing: Integrating a number of different positions containing diverse information and conclusions into a new, single, inclusive position that all group members can agree on and commit themselves to.

Team: A set of interpersonal relationships structured to achieve established goals.

Team building: The analysis of work procedures and activities to improve productivity, relationships among members, the social competence of members, and the ability of the team to adapt to changing conditions and demands.

Theory: A set of interrelated hypotheses or propositions concerning a phenomenon or set of phenomena.

Threat: The statement that if unless you do as I want you to, I will engage in an act that will harm you. One individual informing another that negative actions will follow if the recipient of the threat does (or does not) behave in some manner. A negotiator stating that unless the other agrees to the proposed settlement, the negotiator will make sure the other is harmed.

Tie-in: In negotiations, an issue considered extraneous by the other person is introduced and you offer to accept a certain settlement provided this extraneous issue will also be settled to one's satisfaction.

Total quality management: Use of teams to continuously improve the processes by which the product or service is produced.

Transactional approach to leadership: An approach suggesting that leadership involves a complex social relationship between leaders and followers in which each exerts influence on the other.

Trust: Perception that a choice can lead to gains or losses, that whether you will gain or lose depends on the behavior of the other person, that the loss will be greater than the gain, and that the person will likely behave so that you will gain rather than lose.

Trusting behavior: Openness and sharing.

Trustworthy behavior: Expressing acceptance, support, and cooperative intentions.

Unitary Task: Cannot be divided into subtasks. One person has to complete the entire task.

Victim derogation: The tendency for persons who take unfair advantage of others to view negatively the victims of their exploitation, believing that the victims somehow **deserve** such treatment.

Triggering event: An event (such as two group members being in competition or the expression of criticism on a sensitive point) that triggers the occurrence of a conflict.

Win-lose dynamic: Seeing every action of the other as a move to dominate.

Zeitgeist: Spirit or temper of the times.